CLASSIC
CHRISTIANITY
STUDY
SERIES

A Closer Look at
Faith, Hope
& Love

BOB
GEORGE

PEOPLE TO PEOPLE MINISTRIES
2300 Valley View Ln. #200 Dallas, Texas 75234
(972) 620-1755

A CLOSER LOOK AT FAITH, HOPE & LOVE

PEOPLE TO PEOPLE MINISTRIES
2300 Valley View Ln. #200 Dallas, Texas 75234
(972) 620-1755

ISBN 1-56507-175-1

Printed in the United States of America.

94   95   96   97   98   99   00   —   10   9   8   7   6   5   4   3   2   1

Contents

No Other Foundation

As a person's physical growth is based on proper diet and exercise, so a Christian's spiritual growth depends on regular feeding upon the Word of God and application of its truth. With more false teaching, shifting opinions, and general confusion in the world than ever before, Christians need a solid foundation upon which to base their beliefs and build their lives. The Word of God declares that Jesus Christ is that foundation of truth. Therefore the emphasis of the Classic Christianity Study Series is in helping Christians discover for themselves what the Bible actually says about Christ.

These Bible study guides are uniquely prepared for this purpose. They are useful for the newborn, intermediate, or mature Christian in that they begin with the fundamental and central question of who Jesus Christ is and then build upon that foundation in a logical and progressive manner. The Classic Christianity Study Series is also extremely flexible in that it can be used for individual or group study.

The book of Acts tells us that the first Christians were "continually devoting themselves to the apostles' *teaching* and to *fellowship*, to the *breaking of bread* and to *prayer*" (Acts 2:42 NASB). The need for a proper balance in the Christian life is as real today as it was in the first century. The Classic Christianity Study Series has therefore been designed to incorporate all of these elements vital for spiritual growth.

> *No man can lay a foundation other than the one which is laid, which is Jesus Christ* (1 Corinthians 3:11 NASB).

Helpful Suggestions
As You Begin

1. Choose a convenient time and location. This will help you to be consistent in your study.

2. Use a Bible that you are comfortable with.

3. Before beginning your study, always ask God to quiet your heart and open your mind to understand the Scriptures.

4. Approach the Word of God with a learner's heart and a teachable spirit.

1

But Now Abide . . .

Throughout the apostle Paul's epistles you find him commending and encouraging his fellow Christians for their faith, hope, and love. The Christian life is lived by faith, encouraged by hope, and exemplified by love. The New Testament points out these qualities as being the Christian's criteria for evaluating his or her ongoing spiritual maturity, and the evidence to an unbelieving world of a living Lord and a living faith.

Each of these qualities is treated as a separate subject in this book. But this chapter will show that faith, hope, and love are linked together. A person cannot experience the love of God or love for others apart from faith and hope. The same is true for experiencing faith and hope. So as you work through each chapter remember that faith, hope, and love work together in our lives and enable us to experience the abundant life that Jesus promised.

With this in mind let us take a closer look at faith, hope, and love.

Key Verse: 1 Corinthians 13:13

Now these three remain: faith, hope and love. But the greatest of these is love.

According to 1 Corinthians 13 . . .

1. Prophecies will cease, tongues will be stilled, and knowledge will pass away, but what three things will remain?

2. Of these three, which is the greatest?

3. In your opinion, why does this verse say that love is the greatest?

4. Since these three things remain, what can you conclude about God's priorities for a Christian?

5. Since Paul groups these three qualities together, do you think they may be interdependent?

According to Ephesians 1:15-18 . . .

1. What two things did Paul give thanks for concerning the Christians at Ephesus?

2. Who was their faith in and their love expressed to?

3. Why did Paul pray that the eyes of their hearts might be enlightened?

4. How did Paul describe the hope that we have as Christians?

> *We always thank God, the Father of our Lord Jesus Christ, when we pray for you, because we have heard of your faith in Christ Jesus and of the love you have for all the saints—the faith and love that spring from the hope that is stored up for you in heaven and that you have already heard about in the word of truth, the gospel that has come to you. All over the world this gospel is bearing fruit and growing, just as it has been doing among you since the day you heard it and understood God's grace in all its truth* (Colossians 1:3-6).

1. What two things did Paul thank the Lord for concerning the Colossian Christians?

2. According to this passage, where did this faith and love spring from?

3. Where had the Colossians heard about this hope that is stored up for them in heaven?

4. What did Paul say this gospel was doing all over the world?

5. When did this gospel start bearing fruit in their lives?

> *We always thank God for all of you, mentioning you in our prayers. We continually remember before our God and Father your work produced by faith, your labor prompted by love, and your endurance inspired by hope in our Lord Jesus Christ* (1 Thessalonians 1:2,3).

1. What three things did Paul continually remember before God in his prayers?

2. What produced the work that Paul mentioned, according to these verses?

3. What prompted their labor among the saints?

4. What inspired their endurance?

According to 1 Thessalonians 5:4-11 . . .

1. Paul was writing to the Thessalonians about the coming of the Lord. He said this day should not surprise us as Christians. What reason did he give?

2. As Christians, are we sons of the night or sons of the day?

3. Because we are sons of the light, how does Paul tell us to live?

4. Paul says that we should be alert and self-controlled. How does he say we should accomplish this?

5. What protection do faith, hope, and love provide for us as Christians?

6. What is truth for those of us who are in Christ, whether we are awake or asleep?

7. Therefore, how should we treat one another?

8. How do you see faith, hope, and love at work together in this passage?

> *By faith we eagerly await through the Spirit the righteousness for which we hope. For in Christ Jesus neither circumcision nor uncircumcision has any value. The only thing that counts is faith expressing itself through love* (Galatians 5:5,6).

1. According to this verse, what do we eagerly await by faith?

2. What is the only thing that counts in this life?

3. Do you think our faith could express itself through love apart from knowing the hope that we have in Christ?

4. In all of the verses that we have read, what is the relationship between faith, hope, and love?

A number of years ago I did not understand the relationship between faith, hope, and love. I was trying to write a study guide on love. Because of my lack of understanding of how these three qualities work together, it turned out to be a very frustrating experience. I thought I knew all about love, but through that experience I discovered I actually knew very little about love.

It was through the very passages of Scripture we have studied in this chapter that my eyes were opened to the importance of the relationship between faith, hope, and love. As I started examining these three qualities, I began to see the complete picture of what the Christian life is all about.

You cannot separate faith, hope, and love. It is my prayer that as you learn what faith, hope, and love are, and see how they work together, you will see and experience the fullness of the Christian life.

Since we enter the Christian life through faith, our next chapter takes a closer look at faith.

2

Faith Defined

When talking about faith, we are talking about dependence. Someone once said, "Faith is an action taken on the part of man toward a promise made by God." We can trust what God says in His Word. To walk by faith means to walk in dependence not only on the written Word, but also on the living Word, who is Christ. Faith is a conscious choice to believe and trust what He said and did on our behalf.

The New Testament consistently tells us first who we are, then exhorts us to present ourselves to God in dependent faith. Learning to walk in these truths does not happen overnight; it requires the ongoing ministry of the Holy Spirit through the Scriptures.

Key Verse: Hebrews 11:1

Faith is being sure of what we hope for and certain of what we do not see.

---

1. How does this verse define faith?

2. What do we hope for?

3. Why do you think the writer of this verse made the point to define faith as being certain of what we do not *see*?

4. According to Hebrews 11:1, can we walk by faith and sight at the same time?

> *Without faith it is impossible to please God, because anyone who comes to him must believe that he exists and that he rewards those who earnestly seek him* (Hebrews 11:6).

1. What is it that makes it impossible to please God?

2. What must we believe about God?

3. Is it enough to simply believe that God exists?

4. To truly have exercised faith, what must we believe God will do for those who seek Him?

5. What is God's reward to those who earnestly seek Him?

Faith Is Not a Feeling

Faith and feelings are two different things. Faith is a response to the truth of God's Word. Feelings are a response to what we have taken into our minds through our five senses—what we see, hear, smell, taste, and feel. Feelings have no intellect. They cannot differentiate between past, present, or future; they are unable to distinguish between reality and fantasy, truth or lies. Feelings are never initiators. They merely *respond* to whatever a person is thinking.

Many Christians have adopted the byline of today's generation: "If it feels good, do it!" There is no consistency, however, in a faith based on feelings, and such a faith inevitably results in a "spiritual roller coaster" experience. If a Christian continually seeks spiritual experiences apart from the Word of God, he will become fanatical and undisciplined, having "a zeal for God, but not in accordance with knowledge" (Romans 10:2 NASB).

Faith, however, is based on truth which never changes. It is interesting to observe that the Bible is almost silent about the subject of feelings, but faith is covered from Genesis to Revelation. Rather than waiting to "get excited" or to "feel like it," we are to respond by faith to the truth of God's Word. Then we will experience a quality of life that transcends our feelings—a life characterized by love, joy, peace, patience, kindness, goodness, gentleness, and self-control.

> *By faith Abraham, when called to go to a place he would later receive as his inheritance, obeyed and went, even though he did not know where he was going* (Hebrews 11:8).

1. What was Abraham's response when God called him to go to the land that he would later receive as an inheritance?

2. Did he know where he was going?

3. Do you think Abraham felt good about moving his family to a strange new land?

4. What do you think Abraham learned about God after he received what was promised?

5. Was Abraham's faith based on a feeling or on the truth about God?

Do not worry about tomorrow, for tomorrow will worry about itself.
Each day has enough trouble of its own (Matthew 6:34).

1. What does Jesus tell us not to worry about?

2. When we worry about tomorrow, how do we feel today?

3. Is it possible to worry and have faith at the same time?

4. Since we don't know what will happen tomorrow, does it make sense to worry about it?

5. If not, what is the only other alternative?

Brothers, I do not consider myself yet to have taken hold of it. But one thing I do: Forgetting what is behind and straining toward what is ahead, I press on toward the goal to win the prize for which God has called me heavenward in Christ Jesus (Philippians 3:13,14).

1. What does Paul say we should do with our past?

2. How does thinking about the past control how we feel today?

3. Can our emotions discern the past, present, or future?

4. Since we can't change our past, what good does it do to dwell on it?

5. What should be our goal in life?

6. Can we see the prize to which God has called us?

> He said to me, "My grace is sufficient for you, for my power is made perfect in weakness." Therefore I will boast all the more gladly about my weaknesses, so that Christ's power may rest on me (2 Corinthians 12:9).

1. What does Paul say is sufficient in the verse?

2. When is this grace sufficient—in the past, present, or future?

3. Where do our minds need to be in order to draw on the sufficiency of God's grace?

4. What does it mean to have faith in the grace of God?

Faith Is an Attitude of Dependence

Dependence is a common word to most of us. In today's world there is much talk about being dependent on something. Whether it is drugs, alcohol, or another person, being dependent means relying on something to give you meaning and purpose in life. As Christians, we depend on Christ for our meaning and purpose in life.

Jesus Christ demonstrated this mind-set by walking in total dependence upon His Father while He was on the earth. Although He was fully God, He behaved as a man. As a result, we can see how we too are to live a life of dependence.

As the Father Has Sent Me, I Am Sending You

Jesus said, "When you have lifted up the Son of Man, then you will know that I am the one I claim to be and that I do nothing on my own but speak just what the Father has taught me (John 8:28).

1. What was Jesus referring to when He said, "When you have lifted up the Son of Man"?

2. What was the source of Jesus' words?

3. Who taught Him what to say?

4. What attitude was He demonstrating?

I did not speak of my own accord, but the Father who sent me commanded me what to say and how to say it. I know that his command leads to eternal life. So whatever I say is just what the Father has told me to say (John 12:49,50).

1. Who commanded Jesus what to say?

2. Did Christ say anything of His own human reasoning?

3. What do God's commands lead to?

4. How dependent was Christ on the Father?

5. How dependent should we be?

> *Jesus gave them this answer: "I tell you the truth, the Son can do nothing by himself; he can do only what he sees his Father doing, because whatever the Father does the Son also does. For the Father loves the Son and shows him all he does. Yes, to your amazement he will show him even greater things than these. . . . By myself I can do nothing; I judge only as I hear, and my judgment is just, for I seek not to please myself but him who sent me* (John 5:19,20,30).

1. What could the Son do apart from the Father?

2. What did the Father show Christ?

3. Did Christ seek to please Himself or God?

4. What can we do apart from the Father?

> *Don't you believe that I am in the Father, and that the Father is in me? The words I say to you are not just my own. Rather, it is the Father, living in me, who is doing his work. Believe me when I say that I am in the Father and the Father is in me; or at least believe on the evidence of the miracles themselves* (John 14:10,11).

1. Where was the Father in relation to Christ?

2. When Christ was on the earth, who was doing the work through Him?

3. If we are in Christ, where does He dwell?

4. Who then should do the work through us?

Faith Means Being Available

God wants us to know Him and love Him, and to trust Him in our daily lives just as we trusted Him for salvation. He also wants us to be available to Him. As we have just seen in the previous verses, Jesus was available to His Father. He described His life as "the Father, living in me, who is doing His work." Along with dependency, availability is a key ingredient to faith.

> *As Jesus was coming up out of the water, he saw heaven being torn open and the Spirit descending on him like a dove. And a voice came from heaven: "You are my Son, whom I love; with you I am well pleased"* (Mark 1:10,11).

1. What did God say about Jesus at His baptism?

2. At this point in Jesus' life, had He healed anyone, performed any miracles, or preached any sermons?

3. Do you think He was available to do so if His Father wanted Him to?

4. What made Jesus pleasing to His Father—what He did or who He was?

5. What makes you pleasing to God—what you do or who you are?

> *Therefore, I urge you, brothers, in view of God's mercy, to offer your bodies as living sacrifices, holy and pleasing to God—this is your spiritual act of worship* (Romans 12:1).

1. What is God's definition of worship?

2. The offering of our bodies to God is in view of what?

3. How do we offer ourselves as living sacrifices?

4. What does God do with these living sacrifices?

God is looking for men, women, boys, and girls who will say, "Lord Jesus, here I am. Apart from You I can do nothing, but I'm presenting myself to You for whatever You are pleased to do through me. I know I can trust You with the results, and to complete the work You began in me." This is true faith. It is a simple trust and dependence on Christ, who is alive and active in all those who are available to Him.

3

The Object
of Our Faith

There is much talk today about having "great faith." But faith by itself is useless. It doesn't matter how much faith you have if it is not placed in an object that is faithful, or worthy of your faith. So the real issue isn't *how much faith* a person has, but rather *the object of that faith.*

Someone could say, "Swallowing makes you live," and that sounds right. Swallowing food does enable me to live. However, I could also swallow poison and die. So it isn't the swallowing itself that nourishes me. It is *what I am swallowing* that gives strength to my body.

Faith is like swallowing. It is not my faith, but the *object* of my faith that saves me.

Key Verses: 2 Peter 1:3,4

His divine power has given us everything we need for life and godliness through our knowledge of him who called us by his own glory and goodness. Through these he has given us his very great and precious promises, so that through them you may participate in the divine nature and escape the corruption in the world caused by evil desires.

1. What has God's divine power given us?

2. This comes from the knowledge of what?

3. What is the result of trusting in His "very great and precious promises"?

4. Is the focus of this verse on faith or the object of our faith?

> *My message and my preaching were not with wise and persuasive words, but with a demonstration of the Spirit's power, so that your faith might not rest on men's wisdom, but on God's power* (1 Corinthians 2:4,5).

1. What was Paul's preaching of the gospel a demonstration of?

2. Why didn't Paul use wise and persuasive words?

3. Therefore, what is the object of faith in this verse?

4. What is our faith to rest in?

> *You have so little faith. I tell you the truth, if you have faith as small as a mustard seed, you can say to this mountain, "Move from here to there" and it will move. Nothing will be impossible for you* (Matthew 17:20).

1. How much faith is Jesus talking about in this verse?

2. According to this verse, how important is the size of a person's faith?

3. Do you know anyone who has moved a mountain?

4. Was Jesus pointing His hearers to their own faith or to the object of their faith?

5. If it was God's desire to move a mountain, how much faith would you need?

> *That is why I am suffering as I am. Yet I am not ashamed, because I know whom I have believed, and am convinced that he is able to guard what I have entrusted to him for that day* (2 Timothy 1:12).

1. Why did Paul say he was not ashamed of his suffering?

2. What was he convinced of?

3. What had Paul entrusted to the Lord?

4. What was the object of Paul's faith?

> *In him you were also circumcised, in the putting off of the flesh, not with a circumcision done by the hands of men but with the circumcision done by Christ, having been buried with him in baptism and raised with him through your faith in the power of God, who raised him from the dead* (Colossians 2:11,12).

1. Who raised Jesus from the dead?

2. Who raises us with Him?

3. What, therefore, is our faith in?

Faith in the Word of God

The Bible is more than just a book; it is the very words of God. God gave us the Word to point us to Christ. As Christ Himself said in John 5:39, "You diligently study the Scriptures because you think that by them you possess eternal life. These are the Scriptures that testify about me." Our primary reason for putting our faith in God's Word is not because of its accuracy or even its power to change lives. The supreme reason for accepting the Bible as inspired by God is our faith in Jesus Christ.

> *You have been born again, not of perishable seed, but of imperishable, through the living and enduring word of God. . . . But the word of the Lord stands forever. And this is the word that was preached to you* (1 Peter 1:23,25).

1. According to this verse, how are we born again?

2. What does Peter say about the Word of God?

3. According to the above verses, what is the object of our faith?

> *All Scripture is God-breathed and is useful for teaching, rebuking, correcting and training in righteousness, so that the man of God may be thoroughly equipped for every good work* (2 Timothy 3:16,17).

1. Where does Scripture come from?

2. How much of it?

3. What is it useful for?

4. What is the result of the truth of God's Word being used in someone's life?

5. What is it that equips us for good works?

6. What should be the focus of our faith?

    It is not how much faith we have that is important. In fact, to emphasize the amount of a person's faith is an insult to God. Rather, the issue is *the greatness and awesome power of the God in whom we believe*. The issue is the *object* of our faith. The object of the Christian's faith is the Lord Jesus Christ and His Word.

4

Examples
of Faith

Key Verse: Romans 1:17

In the gospel a righteousness from God is revealed, a righteousness that is by faith from first to last, just as it is written: "The righteous will live by faith."

---

1. What is revealed in the gospel?

2. Where does this righteousness come from? How is it obtained?

3. How do the righteous live, according to this verse?

   The righteous live by faith. The righteous are those who have put their trust in Jesus Christ and have received His righteousness. The Bible chronicles the lives of many of these believers. Let's take a closer look at several of these people to learn more of what true faith is from their example.

According to Romans 4:18-24 . . .

1. What did Abraham become through his faith?

2. What was the promise that was given to him?

3. What fact did he face concerning his age and his wife Sarah's age?

4. Did the fact that his body was as good as dead weaken his faith?

5. Did he waver in unbelief regarding the promise of God?

6. What happened to Abraham regarding his faith?

7. What was Abraham fully persuaded that God could do?

8. As a result what was credited to him?

9. Were the words "It was credited to him" just for Abraham alone, or were they for us also?

10. How is righteousness credited to us?

11. How is Abraham an example of faith?

12. Who was his faith truly in?

13. Does the basis of Abraham becoming the father of many nations rest on his faith or on God's faithfulness to keep His promise? (See Genesis 12:1-3 to see what God promised.)

> *By faith Abraham, when God tested him, offered Isaac as a sacrifice. He who had received the promises was about to sacrifice his one and only son, even though God had said to him, "It is through Isaac that your offspring will be reckoned." Abraham reasoned that God could raise the dead, and figuratively speaking, he did receive Isaac back from death* (Hebrews 11:17-19).

1. By faith what did Abraham do, according to this passage?

2. What had God said to Abraham concerning his son Isaac?

3. What did Abraham reason that God could do?

4. What then enabled Abraham to offer Isaac as a sacrifice?

5. How is this an example of faith for us?

According to Hebrews 11:32-38 . . .

1. The writer of Hebrews did not have time to mention all the other saints who walked by faith, but he did mention what was accomplished through these men and women of God. From verses 33-35 list what these people accomplished through faith.

2. In verses 36-38 list what others accomplished through their faith.

3. According to these verses, is walking by faith dependent upon the circumstances you are in?

4. Can you walk by faith while conquering kingdoms and administering justice just as easily as you can walk by faith in the midst of being beaten, chained, sawed, or stoned?

5. What circumstance are you currently facing, and does this circumstance prohibit you from walking by faith in Jesus Christ?

According to 1 Timothy 1:15-17 . . .

1. What is the trustworthy saying that deserves our full acceptance?

2. Why was Paul shown mercy?

3. What did Jesus Christ display to you and me through His relationship with Paul?

4. How was this an example to us?

5. To whom did Paul give glory and honor as a result?

> *I am already being poured out like a drink offering, and the time has come for my departure. I have fought the good fight, I have finished the race, I have kept the faith. Now there is in store for me the crown of righteousness, which the Lord, the righteous Judge, will award to me on that day—and not only to me, but also to all who have longed for his appearing* (2 Timothy 4:6-8).

1. At what point in Paul's life was he writing these words?

2. How did he describe the way he had lived his life?

3. What was in store for him?

4. What is in store for us who long for Christ's appearing just as Paul did?

5. Throughout Paul's life he persevered through thick and thin. How does his perseverance encourage you to continue fighting the good fight and to finish the race that is set before you?

> *To this you were called, because Christ suffered for you, leaving you an example, that you should follow in his steps. "He committed no sin, and no deceit was found in his mouth." When they hurled their insults at him, he did not retaliate; when he suffered, he made no threats. Instead, he entrusted himself to him who judges justly* (1 Peter 2:21-23).

1. According to this passage, we were called to follow Christ's example of suffering. In the midst of people hurling insults, what did He do?

2. How then should we follow in His steps when we receive insults and suffer just as He did?

3. In whom should we place our faith in the midst of the circumstances of life?

According to Hebrews 12:1,2 . . .

1. After listing the great men and women of faith and what they accomplished, the writer of Hebrews says their example should encourage us to do what?

2. How should we run the race that is marked out for us?

3. What should we fix our eyes on?

4. How do these verses describe Jesus?

5. What was the example that He gave us through His life?

Abraham, Paul, and the other people mentioned in the book of Hebrews are considered great heroes of the faith. Scripture says that each of these people accomplished great things through their faith. But as we have examined their lives, we have seen that their stories are not about what they accomplished, but what God accomplished through them. Their faith was merely a deep conviction held in the heart that God was able to do exactly what He promised. And so it is with us.

God recorded the lives of these people to serve as examples of what it means to live by faith. We are not to try to be exactly like them. Their lives encourage us to walk by faith in the midst of whatever circumstances we face in life. Like these people, we are to have a deep conviction that regardless of what this life brings, God is able to do exactly what He promised us.

The same God who worked through these people is alive and living in the hearts of His people today. Keep your eyes on Him and live with utter certainty that He will complete the work that He began in you. As you do, like Abraham and Paul, your life will become an example of what faith truly is.

5

Faith
Lived Out

Faith always views problems as opportunities to trust God. Victorious Christian living never comes from simply understanding our problems; victory comes from *claiming God's promises*.

In the midst of problems and frustrations, Christ can be trusted to work all things together for our good. Since we know this in advance, faith always says "Thank You." No matter what happens, we can place our faith in Christ to carry us through this life.

Key Verse: 1 Thessalonians 5:18

Give thanks in all circumstances, for this is God's will for you in Christ Jesus.

1. In how many circumstances are we to give thanks?

2. What is God's will for us in Christ Jesus?

3. Are we to give thanks *for* the circumstance or *in* the circumstance?

4. What enables us to give thanks?

> *... always giving thanks to God the Father for everything, in the name of our Lord Jesus Christ* (Ephesians 5:20).

1. Who are we to thank in all situations, and whose name are we to do it in?

2. What is the significance of giving thanks in Jesus' name?

3. Is giving thanks for God's benefit or our own?

> *We know that in all things God works for the good of those who love him, who have been called according to his purpose. . . . He who did not spare his own Son, but gave him up for us all—how will he not also, along with him, graciously give us all things?* (Romans 8:28,32).

1. In what things does God work for our good?

2. According to these verses, what did God give us?

3. Did God hold anything back when He gave us Christ?

4. Is there anything He will hold back from us now if we are in Him?

5. Would you say that God always has our best in mind?

6. Does knowing this promise of God enable you to give thanks in all things?

> *Who of you by worrying can add a single hour to his life? Since you cannot do this very little thing, why do you worry about the rest?* (Luke 12:25,26).

1. Can worrying benefit your life in any way?

2. What does worrying produce in your life?

3. Does anybody know what will happen in the future?

4. Does it make much sense to worry about something that you have no control over?

5. Can you worry and have faith in God at the same time?

> *Do not be anxious about anything, but in everything, by prayer and petition, with thanksgiving, present your requests to God. And the peace of God, which transcends all understanding, will guard your hearts and your minds in Christ Jesus* (Philippians 4:6,7).

1. What should be our attitude when we are feeling anxious?

2. Who are we to present our concerns to?

3. What is the result of trusting God in your circumstances and thanking Him in the midst of them?

4. Can the peace of God be understood with our minds?

5. What will the peace of God do for our hearts and minds?

> *The mind of sinful man is death, but the mind controlled by the Spirit is life and peace* (Romans 8:6).

1. What is the mind of sinful man set on?

2. What is the mind controlled by the Spirit set on?

3. How can we let our minds be controlled by the Holy Spirit?

4. When our minds are controlled by the Spirit, who is our faith in?

Living It Out

The Bible tells us that if we have something against our brother we are to go to him and straighten it out. Usually this is not our first response to this type of problem. We believe that following this advice may cause further problems, and besides, confrontation is not pleasant for any of us.

However, faith always believes that God will cause all things to work together for good, and it produces obedience to His Word. We can trust God with the results. All He asks is that we do what He says. As we walk in faith our relationships are restored, and what we believed would turn out for the worst, God uses for our good.

According to Romans 12:17-21 . . .

1. What is usually our first response when someone has wronged us?

2. How does God say we should handle the matter?

3. Can you control another person's attitude toward you?

4. How are we to overcome evil?

5. Can God be trusted to deal with others who have hurt us?

> *You, my brothers, were called to be free. But do not use your freedom to indulge the flesh; rather, serve one another in love* (Galatians 5:13).

1. What were we called to be?

2. What are we to use this freedom to do?

3. What does it mean to be free in Christ?

4. Can you be indulging your flesh and serving someone in love at the same time?

Faith in Christ allows us to say "Thank You" in every circumstance. Are there circumstances in your life for which you have been unwilling to give thanks?

Are you willing to trust God with every aspect of your life, and thank Him confidently that He will "cause all things to work for your good"?

6

The Christian's Hope

God not only provided a life of spiritual abundance for us here on earth, but also a life of total freedom from sin for all eternity. God has asked us to spend a short period of time here on earth serving Him in the midst of sin in exchange for spending eternity with Him totally free from its presence.

The Christian's hope lies in the truth that this world and its problems will soon pass away. In light of eternity, the problems and circumstances that we all face on a daily basis begin to lose their magnitude. The biblical promise of our future home gives us hope to face tomorrow.

Key Verses: 1 John 3:1-3

How great is the love the Father has lavished on us, that we should be called children of God! And that is what we are! The reason the world does not know us is that it did not know him. Dear friends, now we are children of God, and what we will be has not yet been made known. But we know that when he appears, we shall be like him, for we shall see him as he is. Everyone who has this hope in him purifies himself, just as he is pure.

---

1. What has the Father lavished on us?

2. What are we now called?

3. Is this just a name or is this what we really are?

4. As children of God, what shall we someday become?

5. What is the result when a Christian lives with this hope in his heart?

> *In my Father's house are many rooms; if it were not so, I would have told you. I am going there to prepare a place for you. And if I go and prepare a place for you, I will come back and take you to be with me that you also may be where I am* (John 14:2,3).

1. What is Christ referring to when he says "my Father's house"?

2. Since Christ's work in regard to our salvation is complete, what is He doing for us until He returns?

3. What will He do when He comes again?

According to 1 Thessalonians 4:13-18 . . .

1. What is our hope as Christians?

2. Why did Paul write this passage?

3. Describe the events surrounding the Lord's appearing.

4. What are you to do with the hope of the Lord's return?

> *Therefore we do not lose heart. Though outwardly we are wasting away, yet inwardly we are being renewed day by day. . . . We fix our eyes not on what is seen, but on what is unseen. For what is seen is temporary, but what is unseen is eternal* (2 Corinthians 4:16,18).

1. What is the believer to fix his eyes on?

2. How can we fix our eyes on something we can't see?

3. What does Paul say about the things that we *can* see? About the things we *can't* see?

4. If the things we *can* see are only temporary, why do we spend so much time focusing on them?

> *We know that the whole creation has been groaning as in the pains of childbirth right up to the present time. Not only so, but we ourselves, who have the firstfruits of the Spirit, groan inwardly as we wait eagerly for our adoption as sons, the redemption of our bodies. For in this hope we were saved. But hope that is seen is no hope at all. Who hopes for what he already has? But if we hope for what we do not yet have, we wait for it patiently* (Romans 8:22-25).

1. What is it that causes us to "groan inwardly"?

2. What are we eagerly awaiting?

3. Can we see this hope?

4. If we could see it, would it still be hope?

5. On what basis can we put our hope in something that we can't see?

> *Listen, I tell you a mystery: We will not all sleep, but we will all be changed—in a flash, in the twinkling of an eye, at the last trumpet. For the trumpet will sound, the dead will be raised imperishable, and we will be changed. . . . When the perishable has been clothed with the imperishable, and the mortal with immortality, then the saying that is written will come true: "Death has been swallowed up in victory." "Where, O death, is your victory? Where, O death, is your sting?" The sting of death is sin, and the power of sin is the law. But thanks be to God! He gives us the victory through our Lord Jesus Christ* (1 Corinthians 15:51-57).

1. When will we be changed?

2. What will happen to our mortal bodies?

3. Will death have any mastery over us?

4. What is the sting of death?

5. Where is the power of sin?

6. How are we victorious over sin and the law?

7. With these things in mind, how does 1 Corinthians 15:51-57 encourage us concerning death?

> *Since everything will be destroyed in this way, what kind of people ought you to be? You ought to live holy and godly lives as you look forward to the day of God and speed its coming. That day will bring about the destruction of the heavens by fire, and the elements will melt in the heat. But in keeping with his promise we are looking forward to a new heaven and a new earth, the home of righteousness* (2 Peter 3:11-13).

1. What will ultimately happen to this world?

2. In light of this fact, what should our attitude be?

3. Will believers be destroyed as well? What is our final destiny?

4. Who will dwell in the new heaven and the new earth?

As surely as God's Word is true, one of these days—and it could be today—Jesus will come, and all who know Him will rise to meet Him in the air. We should live in this blessed hope and expectation of our Lord's return.

Our hope of Christ's return enables us to see life in light of eternity and set our priorities accordingly. It is our paramount motivation for understanding the Lord's words to "seek first his kingdom and his righteousness" (Matthew 6:33). All things we see today will someday vanish; only those things we cannot see will remain forever. This is the believer's hope.

7

Hope for Today

In the previous chapter we looked at the Christian's hope. There we learned about our hope for the future contained within the promises of God—that Christ has gone to prepare a place for us, and that one day we will be like Him when we see Him face-to-face. Our hope as Christians is the most comforting and encouraging news that we could possibly dream or imagine.

Sometimes, however, this hope seems far away. We live in the real world today and face many trials and tribulations. Can we really experience the abundant life that Jesus promised here and now? Let's take a closer look at the Word of God and see the hope that we have for today.

Key Verses: Colossians 1:27,28

To them God has chosen to make known among the Gentiles the glorious riches of this mystery, which is Christ in you, the hope of glory. We proclaim him, admonishing and teaching everyone with all wisdom, so that we may present everyone perfect in Christ.

1. In Colossians 1:23 Paul tells us not to be moved from the hope held out in the gospel. How do the key verses define the hope held out to us in the gospel?

2. What did God choose to make known to us concerning the hope of glory?

3. According to this verse, what is our hope for experiencing the abundant life here and now?

4. What do you think the phrase "hope of glory" means?

5. Who did Paul proclaim and preach as a result of knowing that Christ in us is our hope of glory?

> *Paul, an apostle of Christ Jesus by the command of God our Savior and of Christ Jesus our hope* (1 Timothy 1:1).

1. Who does Paul say is our hope, according to this verse?

2. Who then is our hope for experiencing the abundant life here and today?

> *Praise be to the God and Father of our Lord Jesus Christ! In his great mercy he has given us new birth into a living hope through the resurrection of Jesus Christ from the dead* (1 Peter 1:3).

1. What did God give to us in His great mercy?

2. Is the hope that we have a living hope or a dead hope?

3. What makes our hope living?

4. What was the response Peter had to this living hope we have in Jesus Christ?

> *I do not understand what I do. For what I want to do I do not do, but what I hate I do. And if I do what I do not want to do, I agree that the law is good. As it is, it is no longer I myself who do it, but it is sin living in me* (Romans 7:15-17).

1. How did Paul describe the struggle he experienced?

2. Can you identify with his struggle?

3. Do you have an understanding of why the things you want to do you don't do, and the things you don't want to do you do?

4. Did Paul have an understanding of why he did the things he did?

5. What was his explanation of this bondage?

6. What do you think is our hope for being freed from this bondage of "the things I want to do I do not do, but what I hate I do"?

> *What a wretched man I am! Who will rescue me from this body of death? Thanks be to God—through Jesus Christ our Lord! So then, I myself in my mind am a slave to God's law, but in the sinful nature a slave to the law of sin* (Romans 7:24,25).

1. What did Paul conclude about himself, according to this verse?

2. What was Paul's question?

3. How did he answer this question?

4. How do you see "Christ in you, the hope of glory" as the solution to the things "I want to do I do not do"?

According to Romans 6:10-14 . . .

1. Paul tells us that Christ died for sin once for all, but the life he lives he lives to God. In the same way what are we to do, according to this passage?

2. Who are we alive to?

3. Therefore what does Paul tell us not to let reign in our mortal bodies?

4. Who are we to offer ourselves to?

5. What will our bodies become as we offer ourselves to God?

6. What is the result?

7. Where then is the freedom from sin being our master?

> *The former regulation is set aside because it was weak and useless (for the law made nothing perfect), and a better hope is introduced, by which we draw near to God* (Hebrews 7:18,19).

1. What was set aside, according to this verse?

2. Why was it set aside?

3. What now has been introduced?

4. This better hope enables us to do what?

> *Then he adds: "Their sins and lawless acts I will remember no more." And where these have been forgiven, there is no longer any sacrifice for sin* (Hebrews 10:17,18).

1. The better hope which the writer of Hebrews mentioned is contained in the new covenant. In this new covenant, what does God do concerning our sins and lawless acts?

2. Why then do you think this better hope that has been introduced enables us to draw near to God?

3. How does an understanding of our total forgiveness in Christ enable us to trust Christ living in us today?

> *Live by the Spirit, and you will not gratify the desires of the flesh* (Galatians 5:16).

1. How does Paul tell us to live, according to this verse?

2. What do you think the phrase "live by the Spirit" means?

3. How do you think living by the Spirit relates to the fact that Christ is alive, living in our hearts?

4. What is the result of living by the Spirit, according to this verse?

> *The fruit of the Spirit is love, joy, peace, patience, kindness, good-ness, faithfulness, gentleness and self-control. Against such things there is no law. Those who belong to Christ Jesus have crucified the flesh with its passions and desires* (Galatians 5:22-24).

1. What is the fruit of the Spirit, according to these verses?

2. What then will be produced in our lives as we live by the Spirit?

3. What does this say concerning those who belong to Christ Jesus?

4. Where then does our freedom from sin come from?

> *May our Lord Jesus Christ himself and God our Father, who loved us and by his grace gave us eternal encouragement and good hope, encourage your hearts and strengthen you in every good deed and word* (2 Thessalonians 2:16,17).

1. What did the Lord Jesus Christ give to us?

2. In regard to what Christ gave us, what was Paul's prayer on our behalf?

3. Who does Paul say will strengthen us in every good deed and word?

4. Who then is our hope of experiencing the abundant life here and now?

It is impossible for us to live the Christian life through our self-efforts. Jesus never intended us to. That is why He has come to live in our hearts. As we walk in dependence upon Jesus, we can experience new life. Our hope for eternity rests totally upon Jesus Christ. Our hope for experiencing the abundant life today is "Christ in you, the hope of glory" (Colossians 1:27).

8

Hope
Lived Out

Suppose someone told you as a child that one day in the future you would be the greatest basketball player ever to play the game. Imagine the thrill of thinking, "One day I will be the next Michael Jordan." Every day you would dream of what it would be like—making those last-second game-winning shots, winning the world championship, or averaging 50 or more points per game.

How do you think knowing this would affect your life today? Do you think it would cause you to sit on the couch and waste your life away? No, if you knew you would be the greatest basketball player, you would never want to leave the basketball court. You would enjoy playing the game as much as possible today, anticipating the day when you would be the greatest.

So it is with the hope that we have in Jesus Christ. Knowing that one day we will be like Jesus and will be with Him forever does affect the way we live today. Let's take a look at Scripture and see how our hope expresses itself in our daily lives.

Key Verses: Colossians 1:3-5

We always thank God, the Father of our Lord Jesus Christ, when we pray for you, because we have heard of your faith in Christ Jesus and of the love you have for all the saints—the faith and love that spring from the hope that is stored up for you in heaven and that you have already heard about in the word of truth, the gospel that has come to you.

---

1. Paul thanked God for the faith the Colossian Christians had in Christ and their love for all the saints. Where did this faith and love spring from?

2. How did this hope express itself in their daily lives?

3. Where is the hope that we have stored up for us?

4. Where did the Colossian Christians hear about this hope?

5. How will this hope express itself in your life?

> *Because God wanted to make the unchanging nature of his purpose very clear to the heirs of what was promised, he confirmed it with an oath. God did this so that, by two unchangeable things in which it is impossible for God to lie, we who have fled to take hold of the hope offered to us may be greatly encouraged. We have this hope as an anchor for the soul, firm and secure* (Hebrews 6:17-19).

1. What did God want to make very clear to His heirs?

2. An oath in the Old Testament ended all arguments concerning the validity of a promise. How did God confirm the validity of His promise to us?

3. Why did God do this?

4. Who are those that are greatly encouraged by the oath that God made confirming His promise of eternal life for us?

5. Now that we have this hope, what role does it serve for our souls?

6. What is the purpose of an anchor on a ship?

7. How badly do we need an anchor to keep our souls firm and secure in this world that we live in?

8. Do you see why it is so important to understand the hope that we have as Christians?

According to 1 Timothy 6:17-19 . . .

1. What was Paul's command to those who are rich in this present world?

2. Why are they not to put their hope in wealth?

3. Who are they to put their hope in?

4. What does God provide for us, and for what purpose?

5. Paul also commands the rich "to do good, to be rich in good deeds, and to be generous and willing to share." Could they do so if their hope was in wealth?

6. What does having their hope in God enable them to take hold of?

7. When we have our hope in Christ, what are we able to experience here and today?

> *If the ministry that brought death, which was engraved in letters on stone, came with glory, so that the Israelites could not look steadily at the face of Moses because of its glory, fading though it was, will not the ministry of the Spirit be even more glorious? If the ministry that condemns men is glorious, how much more glorious is the ministry that brings righteousness! For what was glorious has no glory now in comparison with the surpassing glory. And if what was fading away came with glory, how much greater is the glory of that which lasts! Therefore, since we have such a hope, we are very bold* (2 Corinthians 3:7-12).

According to 2 Corinthians 3:7-12 . . .

1. In this passage Paul is comparing the old covenant to the new covenant. How did he describe the ministry that was engraved in letters on stone?

2. Did this ministry come with glory?

3. Was the glory of the old covenant permanent or was its glory fading away?

4. In comparison, what did Paul say about the glory of the ministry of the Spirit?

5. What does the ministry of the Spirit bring?

6. Does the ministry of the Spirit fade away or is it permanent?

7. Since the glory of the ministry of the Spirit is permanent, what did Paul say that he had?

8. What attitude did this hope produce in the life of Paul?

9. What attitudes has your hope in Christ produced in your life?

> *The grace of God that brings salvation has appeared to all men. It teaches us to say "No" to ungodliness and worldly passions, and to live self-controlled, upright and godly lives in this present age, while we wait for the blessed hope—the glorious appearing of our great God and Savior, Jesus Christ* (Titus 2:11-13).

1. How does the grace of God teach us to live here and today?

2. What are we waiting for as we live our lives in this present age?

3. What is our blessed hope?

4. Why did Jesus give Himself for us?

5. If we did not have the hope of the glorious appearing of Jesus Christ, do you think we would allow the grace of God to teach us how to live today?

6. What are the characteristics of the people that Christ has purified for Himself?

7. How then are we, who have the hope of Christ's appearing, to live our lives here on earth?

> *Let us hold unswervingly to the hope we profess, for he who promised is faithful. And let us consider how we may spur one another on toward love and good deeds. Let us not give up meeting together, as some are in the habit of doing, but let us encourage one another—and all the more as you see the Day approaching* (Hebrews 10:23-25).

1. What are we to hold unswervingly to?

2. For what reason can we hold to this hope we profess?

3. Because of this hope that we have now, what should our attitude be toward others?

> *Who is going to harm you if you are eager to do good? But even if you should suffer for what is right, you are blessed. "Do not fear what they fear; do not be frightened." But in your hearts set apart Christ as Lord. Always be prepared to give an answer to everyone who asks you to give the reason for the hope that you have. But do this with gentleness and respect, keeping a clear conscience, so that those who speak maliciously against your good behavior in Christ may be ashamed of their slander* (1 Peter 3:13-16).

1. Peter tells us not to be frightened. What attitude does he tell us to have instead?

2. What should we always be prepared to give as an answer to everyone who asks?

3. How are we to give the reason for the hope we have as children of God?

4. For those that are lost in this world, what is their deepest need?

5. Do you see why it is so important to know the hope that we have in Christ?

I pray also that the eyes of your heart may be enlightened in order that you may know the hope to which he has called you, the riches of his glorious inheritance in the saints (Ephesians 1:18).

1. What did Paul pray concerning the eyes of our heart?

2. What did he want us to know?

3. Did Paul think it is important for us to know the hope that we have as Christians?

4. Why do you think Paul prayed that the eyes of our heart may be enlightened in order that we may know the hope to which we have been called?

5. How does he describe this hope that we have in Christ?

We have learned that from hope springs forth our faith and love. This hope serves as an anchor for our soul, keeping us firm and secure in this world. It is what enables us to be bold and to not fear those who are enemies of the gospel. It also enables us to encourage one another to love and good deeds. Knowing the hope that we have in Christ does change the way we live today. In light of this, are you willing to adopt Paul's prayer in your own life—that God would enlighten the eyes of your heart so that you may know the hope to which you have been called?

9

God's Love for You

There are two words used in the original language of the New Testament for love, the Greek words *phileo* and *agape*. Simply defined, phileo is friendship love (e.g. *Phil*adelphia—city of brotherly love, and *phil*anthropic—love of mankind). Phileo is a conditional love based on the actions, character, or lovability of the object. Agape, on the other hand, is unconditional love. It is not based upon the character of the one being loved, but on the character of the one expressing love. Agape loves whether the person is deserving or not because it has chosen to love. This is the kind of love God has for us.

By sending His only Son to die for our sins and to give us life, God demonstrated His unconditional love. He continues to love us unconditionally regardless of our behavior or performance. It is vital that we understand His agape love toward us if we are to love others in the same way.

Key Verses: John 3:16,17

For God so loved the world that he gave his one and only Son, that whoever believes in him shall not perish but have eternal life. For God did not send his Son into the world to condemn the world, but to save the world through him.

---

1. How did God demonstrate His love for you?

2. For what purpose did God send His Son?

3. Did Christ come to condemn us for our sin?

> *Love is patient, love is kind. It does not envy, it does not boast, it is not proud. It is not rude, it is not self-seeking, it is not easily angered, it keeps no record of wrongs. Love does not delight in evil but rejoices with the truth. It always protects, always trusts, always hopes, always perseveres. Love never fails. But where there are prophecies, they will cease; where there are tongues, they will be stilled; where there is knowledge, it will pass away* (1 Corinthians 13:4-8).

1. How does Paul define love in this passage?

2. The Bible tells us that God is love. To find out how God loves you, substitute the words "love is" with "God is always" in this passage.

The opposite of love is not hate, as many people would think. The opposite of love is *pride* (see the chart on pages 58-59). Love is always concerned with others, and its focus is outward. Pride is concerned with self, and its focus is always inward.

> *We have not received the spirit of the world but the Spirit who is from God, that we may understand what God has freely given us* (1 Corinthians 2:12).

1. What have we received from God?

2. According to this verse, what does His Spirit do in our lives?

3. What must we have to understand the love of God?

God's Definition of Love

God is love and He has defined Himself and His attitude toward us in the thirteenth chapter of 1 Corinthians. *Agape* love is the *attitude* of God expressed in action to man. The opposite attitude of *agape* love is pride.

Read 1 Corinthians 13:4-8 and study the corresponding chart below. Remember that *agape* love can only come from God.

Agape love is . . .	Definition (1 Corinthians 13:4-8)	Pride is . . .
Always patient	Calm self-restraint from punishing others either physically or emotionally for a wrong suffered or for mistakes made. Always forgiving.	Never patient with mistakes. Retaliates when a wrong is suffered.
Always kind	Goodness of heart expressed in actions for another's benefit.	Never kind or interested in another's benefit.
Never jealous or envious	Not being resentfully desirous of another's advantages, possessions, or gifts. Not desirous of another's good that self cannot have.	Always jealous and envious of others' good fortunes.
Never boastful or arrogant	Never seeks to exalt self or is puffed up with pride and self-importance over nothing.	Always boastful and arrogant. Must be the center of attention.
Never acts unbecomingly	Never acts contrary to behavior appropriate to a Christian's position as a child of God, i.e., behaves with modesty, grace, humility, and patience.	Always rude and never considers the feelings of another.

	People to People	
Seeks not its own	Does not insist on having its own way or rights. Looks out for the interest of others.	Always demands its own way and always looks after its own interests.
Not provoked	Never easily stirred to anger; never touchy or quick-tempered.	Always easily provoked; touchy; oversensitive; angry.
Never takes into account a wrong suffered	Bears a wrong without holding it against the one who committed it. Never holds grudges; maintains a forgiving spirit; keeps no record of wrongs.	Always holds grudges and maintains a record of other people's wrongs.
Never rejoices in unrighteousness	Views sin as God does. Is never glad over someone else's mistakes or sins.	Always rationalizes or ignores sin. Rejoices over others' mistakes and sins.
Rejoices with the truth	Rejoices in all that is found in Christ and His Word and in others becoming Christ-like and being used of God.	Never rejoices with the truth and resents others being used of God.
Bears all things	Endures any hardship for another's good. Carries another's burdens.	Never endures anything.
Believes all things	Thinks the best of other people for Christ's sake. Gives others the benefit of the doubt.	Always thinks the worst of others.
Hopes all things	Holds fast to God's promises. Hopes for the best for others.	Doubts God's promises. Hopes for the best for himself alone.
Endures all things	Will last courageously through any trial or span of time with patience and a thankful spirit for the sake of Christ and others.	Never endures trials with patience or faith in Christ. Always complains and resists.

It is the Spirit of God that leads us into all truth. In order to understand the depth of the love of God, we need His Spirit to reveal it to us. It is not something we can comprehend with our own mind or intellect.

> *Do not get drunk on wine, which leads to debauchery. Instead, be filled with the Spirit* (Ephesians 5:18).

> *I pray that out of his glorious riches he may strengthen you with power through his Spirit in your inner being, so that Christ may dwell in your hearts through faith. And I pray that you, being rooted and established in love, may have power, together with all the saints, to grasp how wide and long and high and deep is the love of Christ, and to know this love that surpasses knowledge—that you may be filled to the measure of all the fullness of God* (Ephesians 3:16-19).

1. According to the above verses, what are we to be filled with?

2. What do we need power to understand?

3. Is this a power to *do* something or power to *know* something?

4. Once we know and understand the love of God, what will the end result be?

> *God demonstrates his own love for us in this: While we were still sinners, Christ died for us* (Romans 5:8).

1. How did God demonstrate His love, according to this verse?

2. What were we when Christ died for us?

3. Did we do anything to deserve Christ's forgiveness?

4. According to Jesus in John 15:13, what is the greatest love someone could have for another?

According to Romans 8:35-39 . . .

1. What are the things that cannot separate us from the love of God?

2. What does this tell you about the extent of God's love?

3. Does this love seem conditional on your performance?

4. What was Paul convinced of?

5. Where is the love of God found?

6. If we are abiding in Christ, what else are we abiding in?

For Paul, the love of God was not just a doctrine to be understood but a reality in his own life. When he said in Romans 8:35-39, " I am convinced that . . . [nothing] will be able to separate us from the love of God that is in Christ Jesus our Lord," he had learned this from his own experience. This can be a reality in your life as well. Have you come to understand the extent of God's love for you? If not, ask the Lord to give you the power to understand His love. You might want to pray something like this:

> *Lord Jesus, I pray that You would give me the power to understand how wide and long and high and deep is Your love for me. I ask that You would help me to experience this love so that I will be filled to the measure with Your fullness.*

10

Substitutes for Love

Although we seem to hear more and more talk about love, we see less and less of the reality of love in our daily experience. As a result of our lack of love for one another, we attempt to develop our own definitions and interpretations of what love is, and then diligently try to live up to our own definitions—for example, "Loving Christians will witness for Christ," or "Loving Christians will read the Bible and pray."

The issue becomes "how to become spiritual" rather than the practical New Testament emphasis on "how to love." Love is God-centered and therefore turns our eyes outward to others. A preoccupation with one's own spirituality is self-centered and is therefore all inward: How is my prayer life? How spiritual do I feel? Am I really more spiritual this month than last? We can be absorbed in our own spirituality but be utterly without love.

As stated earlier, the opposite of love is pride. Pride is at the root of any substitute for love. Only God can fill our need for love and acceptance. When that need is not met, we try all kinds of ways to meet that need. "I" becomes the focus of that search, and it is a never-ending cycle of emptiness and longing. Let's look at some of the substitutes for love.

Key Verses: 1 Corinthians 13:1-3

If I speak in the tongues of men and of angels, but have not love, I am only a resounding gong or a clanging cymbal. If I have the gift of prophecy and can fathom all mysteries and all knowledge, and if I have a faith that can move mountains, but have not love, I am nothing. If I give all I possess to the poor and surrender my body to the flames, but have not love, I gain nothing.

---

1. What are some of the substitutes for love mentioned in this verse?

2. How much effort will people exert to do these things?

3. From a human perspective, are these things noble and praiseworthy?

4. How does God value these things apart from love?

5. What are some other "Christian things" that we substitute for love?

According to John 9:13-16 . . .

1. Were the Pharisees glad that the man had received his sight?

2. What were they more concerned about?

3. Would you say they were demonstrating love or pride?

4. Does a preoccupation with observing the law produce love in a person's heart?

5. From God's perspective, what is more important, observing the law or serving someone in love?

According to Luke 10:38-42 . . .

1. What was Martha's attitude toward Mary?

2. What was her attitude toward Jesus?

3. What was Mary's focus on?

4. What was Martha substituting for love?

5. Has there ever been a time in your life when you have substituted service for love?

6. What attitudes were in your heart toward those you were serving?

> *I know your deeds, your hard work and your perseverance. I know that you cannot tolerate wicked men, that you have tested those who claim to be apostles but are not, and have found them false. You have persevered and have endured hardships for my name, and have not grown weary. Yet I hold this against you: You have forsaken your first love* (Revelation 2:2-4).

1. Were the works being done at the church in Ephesus wrong?

2. List some of the good things they were doing.

3. What had they forsaken?

4. What had they substituted for love?

5. Have you ever been so focused on good deeds that you left your first love?

> *Everything in the world—the cravings of sinful man, the lust of his eyes and the boasting of what he has and does—comes not from the Father but from the world. The world and its desires pass away, but the man who does the will of God lives forever* (1 John 2:16,17).

1. Many people substitute earthly things for love. How does this verse describe the desires for earthly things?

2. Where do these cravings come from?

3. What will happen to the world and its desires?

4. What will happen to the person who trusts Christ and does the will of God?

5. Which makes more sense, to trust in Christ and His love or to trust in the things of this world that will one day pass away?

6. When you have put your trust in the things of this world, what happened to the love in your heart?

Am I now trying to win the approval of men, or of God? Or am I trying to please men? If I were still trying to please men, I would not be a servant of Christ (Galatians 1:10).

Many people confuse love with approval. They believe if they can get that special someone—a boss, a parent, a husband, or a wife—to approve of them, then they have their love. This keeps people in the never-ending cycle of trying to gain the approval of others.

1. According to the above verse, what are the only two sources from which you can get approval?

2. Is it possible to be consumed with trying to please people and be serving Christ at the same time?

3. Does the approval of people last very long?

4. Why was winning the approval of people not important to the apostle Paul?

5. If you are in Christ, you are approved of by God. He loves and accepts you unconditionally. Since this is true, does the approval of people really matter?

6. How is our love for others affected when we are seeking their approval?

If you harbor bitter envy and selfish ambition in your hearts, do not boast about it or deny the truth. Such "wisdom" does not come down from heaven but is earthly, unspiritual, of the devil. For where you have

envy and selfish ambition, there you find disorder and every evil prac-
tice. But the wisdom that comes from heaven is first of all pure; then
peace loving, considerate, submissive, full of mercy and good fruit,
impartial and sincere (James 3:14-17).

1. How does James describe the "earthly" wisdom in this verse?

2. Where does this wisdom come from?

3. What is the source of envy and selfish ambition?

4. Where you find envy and selfish ambition, what else do you find?

5. How does James describe the wisdom that comes from heaven?

6. Compare this description of wisdom with the description of love in 1 Corinthians 13.

People are constantly searching for ways to fill the deep longings that ache
within them. No matter how we try to fill this need, we cannot provide the kind
of love and acceptance our hearts are craving. In fact, the Bible tells us that no
matter how hard we try or how much we pretend, our surface joys end in pain and
heartache if the deep longing within us is not satisfied. God wants us to know that
we are already completely loved and accepted by Him. His unconditional love
and grace is the only source that will fill those needs within the human heart.
There are no substitutes.

11

Abiding in Christ's Love

There is clearly a discernible order in the New Testament for how God intended us to live the Christian life:

1. *God's love for us* (1 John 4:10)
   Our knowledge of God's love for us brings about . . .

2. *Our love for God* (1 John 4:19)
   which results in . . .

3. *Our dependency upon God* (John 15:5)
   resulting in . . .

4. *Our obedience to God* (Romans 12:1)

It is only as we approach the teachings of the New Testament in this order that we will find the Christian life falling into place.

Notice in this pattern that our love for God, our dependence upon God, and our obedience to God are the result of knowing God's love for us. It was the love of God demonstrated through Jesus Christ that drew us to Him when we first believed. And it is the love of God that motivates us to walk in total dependence upon Jesus today.

The message of God's unconditional love and grace that He freely gives us in Jesus Christ is what transforms our hearts and lives. That is why the key to the Christian life is learning to abide in God's love.

Key Verse: John 15:9

As the Father has loved me, so have I loved you. Now remain in my love

1. How does Jesus love us?

2. How much do you think the Father loved Jesus?

3. Therefore, how great do you think Jesus' love is for you?

4. What did Jesus tell us to remain or abide in?

To abide in God's love means that you will grow in your understanding of Christ's finished work at the cross.

> *This is how God showed his love among us: He sent his one and only Son into the world that we might live through him. This is love: not that we loved God, but that he loved us and sent his Son as the one who would turn aside his wrath, taking away our sins* (1 John 4:9,10).

1. How did God show His love among us?

2. Why did God send His Son into the world?

3. How do these verses define love?

4. What did God's love do with His wrath?

5. As a result of turning aside God's wrath, what did Christ do with our sins?

6. Once again, if we are going to see God's love for us and remain in that love, where will we have to begin?

> *There is no fear in love. But perfect love drives out fear, because fear has to do with punishment. The one who fears is not made perfect in love* (1 John 4:18).

1. According to this verse, is there any fear in love?

2. What does perfect love do to fear?

3. What does fear have to do with?

4. Can the one who fears be made perfect in love?

5. Have you ever experienced fear and forgotten God's love for you?

6. Because Christ took the punishment for our sins at the cross, is there anything that we have to fear concerning God?

7. Based on this verse, explain why the cross is a demonstration of God's love for us.

> *Love is patient, love is kind. It does not envy, it does not boast, it is not proud. It is not rude, it is not self-seeking, it is not easily angered, it keeps no record of wrongs* (1 Corinthians 13:4,5).

1. According to the definition of love, does love keep records of wrongs?

2. If love did keep records of our wrongs, what would you have to conclude concerning the cross of Jesus Christ, where God demonstrated His love by taking away our sin?

> *By one sacrifice He has made perfect forever those who are being made holy* (Hebrews 10:14).

1. What has God made you, according to this verse?

2. For how long have you been made that way?

3. Were you made perfect through your good works or because of the sacrifice of Jesus Christ?

4. Once again, why do you think the cross is a demonstration of God's love?

5. If you are to abide in God's love, do you see why you will be growing in your understanding of Christ's work on the cross for you?

Abiding in God's love means that you will grow in your understanding of who you are in Christ.

> *You did not receive a spirit that makes you a slave again to fear, but you received the Spirit of sonship. And by him we cry, "Abba, Father." The Spirit himself testifies with our spirit that we are God's children. Now if we are children, then we are heirs—heirs of God and co-heirs with Christ, if indeed we share in his sufferings in order that we may also share in his glory* (Romans 8:15-17).

1. Did we receive a spirit that makes us a slave again to fear?

2. What spirit did we receive?

3. What assurance do we have concerning God's love for us?

4. What does the Spirit of God testify to our human spirit that we are?

5. If we are children, what else are we?

6. Who has granted us our inheritance?

7. Who is our co-heir?

8. Since it was God's love that made us His children, what motivated Him to make us heirs to His riches?

Abiding in God's love is abiding in the vine.

Jesus said, "I am the vine, you are the branches; he who abides in Me, and I in him, he bears much fruit; for apart from Me you can do nothing" (John 15:5 NASB). The reality of Christianity in human experience lies in this simple yet profound statement made by Christ. Christianity does not become practical to us through ceremony, tradition, or even personal moral reform. It is only through abiding in the Vine, the person, the life of Jesus Christ, that we begin to experience a new quality of life.

> *I am the vine; you are the branches. If a man remains in me and I in him, he will bear much fruit; apart from me you can do nothing* (John 15:5).

1. Who is the vine?

2. Who is the branch?

3. What is the responsibility of the branch to the vine?

4. What is the responsibility of the vine to the branch?

5. What is the result of this relationship?

6. Does a branch *produce* fruit or *bear* fruit?

7. How much of the Christian life (fruit) does Christ say you (the branch) can produce apart from Him?

The parable of the vine and the branch is one of the most important teachings in the Bible. Not only did our Lord call us to come to Him—"Come to Me, all who are weary and heavy-laden, and I will give you rest" (Matthew 11:28 NASB)—but He also called us to abide in Him (continually be drawing life from Him) (John 15:5). This abiding relationship enables us to live in complete, everlasting union with the living God, and to experience the daily reality of Christ living His life in and through us.

> *The fruit of the Spirit is love, joy, peace, patience, kindness, goodness, faithfulness, gentleness and self-control. Against such things there is no law* (Galatians 5:22,23).

1. What is the fruit of the Spirit, according to this verse?

2. Is it possible to produce the fruit of the Spirit apart from abiding in the vine?

3. How can we bear the fruit of love toward others?

> *A new command I give you: Love one another. As I have loved you, so you must love one another* (John 13:34).

1. What is the new command that the Lord gave to us?

2. How are we to love others?

3. Is it possible to love others as Christ has loved us through our own efforts?

4. What is the only way we can bear the fruit of love to others and thus fulfill the commandment that Jesus gave to us?

5. How important do you think it is for us to remain or abide in God's love?

Circumstances do not cause your nature; they *reveal* your nature. For example, no one puts anger into you; they merely draw anger out of you. When the soldiers spat upon Christ, plucked out His beard, scourged Him, mocked Him, and finally nailed Him to a cross, what came out of Him? Love, joy, peace, patience, kindness, and forgiveness. Why? Because that was all that was in Him!

Fruit occurs only when a branch is filled to an overflowing capacity with the life of the vine. In the same way, the fruit of the Spirit becomes evident in the life of a believer only when he becomes filled to overflowing with the knowledge of the love and grace of God that is in Christ Jesus.

For example, a person will never be able to love others unconditionally until he is resting in the fullness of God's unconditional love for him. Nor will he express the fruit of peace to others until he himself is filled with the peace of God that surpasses knowledge. Therefore, the work of the believer is not to produce fruit but to abide fully, completely, and continually by faith in the life of the vine. To abide in the vine of Jesus Christ is to live by faith in His continual love and grace toward you.

12

Attitudes of Love

———

God has chosen to use people to express His love and forgiveness to the world. Since actions always follow thought, God is in the process of renewing our minds and giving us the proper attitudes of love. When we understand God's love for us, we begin to see people in a totally new light. We learn to look beyond outward appearances, and begin to see people as God sees them. Having been recipients of God's mercy, kindness, and love ourselves, we begin to extend those same qualities to other people. As we saw in the last chapter, only Christ can produce this kind of love in us. Let's look at the attitudes of love that are necessary to express God's love to others.

Key Verses: Philippians 2:5-8

Your attitude should be the same as that of Christ Jesus: Who, being in very nature God, did not consider equality with God something to be grasped, but made himself nothing, taking the very nature of a servant, being made in human likeness. And being found in appearance as a man, he humbled himself and became obedient to death—even death on a cross!

1. Whose attitude should ours be the same as?

2. What did Christ become?

3. To what point did Christ humble Himself?

4. Was Christ thinking about Himself during any of this?

5. Who did He do it for?

The attitude necessary for expressing God's love involves a continual renewing of the mind.

> *Therefore, I urge you, brothers, in view of God's mercy, to offer your bodies as living sacrifices, holy and pleasing to God—this is your spiritual act of worship. Do not conform any longer to the pattern of this world, but be transformed by the renewing of your mind. Then you will be able to test and approve what God's will is—his good, pleasing and perfect will (Romans 12:1,2).*

1. In light of the above verses, what are we to offer our bodies as?

2. What is this in view of?

3. How does God define "spiritual worship"?

4. What does it mean to be a living sacrifice?

5. How are we transformed?

6. What is the result of a renewed mind?

7. What do you think God's will is concerning our relationships to one another?

We are all members of the body of Christ.

1. According to Romans 12:3-5 how are we instructed to think of ourselves?

2. Does every part of our body have the same function?

3. Do we all serve the same function in the body of Christ?

4. How should our understanding of the body of Christ affect our relationships with other Christians?

Forgive others as Christ has forgiven you.

> As God's chosen people, holy and dearly loved, clothe yourselves with compassion, kindness, humility, gentleness and patience. Bear with each other and forgive whatever grievances you may have against one another. Forgive as the Lord forgave you. And over all these virtues put on love, which binds them all together in perfect unity (Colossians 3:12-14).

1. How are we described in this passage?

2. What are we to "clothe" ourselves with?

3. How are we to forgive others?

4. How did the Lord forgive us?

5. What must be the source if we are to forgive others as the Lord has forgiven us?

Live in peace with all people.

> *If it is possible, as far as it depends on you, live at peace with everyone* (Romans 12:18).

1. How far should we go to live at peace with others?

2. According to this verse, who should we live at peace with?

3. Does this include those who have wronged us?

4. What can motivate the desire to be at peace with all people?

Live to help and serve your brother.

> *Brothers, if someone is caught in a sin, you who are spiritual should restore him gently. But watch yourself, or you also may be tempted* (Galatians 6:1).

1. What are we to do with someone who is trapped in a particular sin?

2. Does this verse say anything about judging or condemning him?

3. What are we to be careful of during this process?

> *Whoever wants to become great among you must be your servant, and whoever wants to be first must be your slave—just as the Son of Man did not come to be served, but to serve, and to give his life as a ransom for many* (Matthew 20:26-28).

1. How does Christ define greatness in this passage?

2. How does this differ from the world's definition?

3. What was Christ's role while on this earth? Should ours be any different?

Love looks at others as what they can become, not as what they are. Remember that we are all in the process of spiritual growth. As someone once put it, "Don't be too hard on me; Christ isn't finished with me yet!"

Surrender your right to always have your own way.

> *He withdrew about a stone's throw beyond them, knelt down and prayed, "Father, if you are willing, take this cup from me; yet not my will, but yours be done"* (Luke 22:41,42).

1. In His humanity, was Christ looking forward to His crucifixion?

2. Was He willing to give up His human desires for the will of God?

3. How should we respond in situations that are a struggle between our emotions and doing the will of God?

4. What was the ultimate outcome of Christ doing the will of the Father?

5. What will be the outcome when we surrender our right to always have our own way?

Surrender your right to always be noticed.

1. According to the parable in Luke 14:7-11, what happens to the person who seeks the place of honor?

2. What happens when we try to always be noticed by others?

3. What attitude does God want to produce in our hearts?

4. Did Christ exalt Himself while He was on the earth?

Surrender your right to pay back evil for evil.

> *You have heard that it was said, "Eye for eye, and tooth for tooth."*
> *But I tell you, Do not resist an evil person. If someone strikes you on the*
> *right cheek, turn to him the other also* (Matthew 5:38,39).

1. What is our first response when someone does something to insult or harm us?

2. How does Christ tell us to respond?

3. In Jesus' day, to strike someone on the cheek was a way of insulting him. How did He respond to those who insulted Him?

4. When we lash out at someone and insult him back, does it ever resolve a situation?

5. Who am I thinking about when I do this?

Surrender your right to expect something in return for loving others.

1. According to Luke 17:7-10, when we are expecting something in return for loving others, who is our focus on?

2. Does it make sense to reward someone for something he is supposed to do?

3. What should be our attitude when loving others?

4. Did Christ expect anything from us after He gave His life?

God has never changed His plan to use His followers to express His love and forgiveness to a lost world. As we grow in our knowledge of the love of God and in appreciation for what Jesus Christ has done for us, His love begins to control us, stirring up in us the desire to give ourselves back to Him. As our minds are then renewed by the truth of the Word of God, He begins to develop proper attitudes of love in us.

Is your mind fixed on His great love for you? Is your attitude of love one that always looks to the interest of others or yourself? Offer yourself to Christ today as a living sacrifice and let Him begin to renew your mind.

13

The Greatest of These

Love is the very nature and character of God. As John tells us, "God is love" (1 John 4:16). That is why Paul could say, "These three remain: faith, hope and love. But the greatest of these is love" (1 Corinthians 13:13).

The measure of the vitality of every Christian is not how much Christian activity he or she is engaged in, but how he is progressing in learning to love others. Jesus summed the Christian life up in these words: "You shall love the Lord your God with all your heart, and with all your soul, and with all your mind . . . [and] you shall love your neighbor as yourself" (Matthew 22:37,39 NASB). Because God first loved us, loving others is to be the lifestyle of every Christian.

As one who belongs to Christ, the Christian has the magnificent privilege of being God's chosen channel through which He pours out the reality of His love and grace to a world hungry for reality. Because the Christian can rest securely in the knowledge of His love and acceptance by a holy God, he is free to look outside himself to the needs of others and be part of the solution to the world's problems rather than part of the problem.

Key Verses: John 13:34,35

A new command I give you: Love one another. As I have loved you, so you must love one another. By this all men will know that you are my disciples, if you love one another.

1. What was the new command that Jesus gave us?

2. How are we to love one another?

3. How is this new command different from the old command—to love your neighbor as yourself?

4. If we are to love others as Christ has loved us, then where must our focus be to fulfill this command?

5. What will all people know we are if we love one another?

6. Why then do you think the greatest of these is love?

> *This is his command: to believe in the name of his Son, Jesus Christ,*
> *and to love one another as he commanded us* (1 John 3:23).

1. What is Jesus' command to us?

2. Can we love one another as He commanded us apart from believing in and trusting in Jesus Christ?

3. Where does the love that we have for others come from?

4. Do you see why God never tells us to love others apart from pointing us back to abiding in His love for us?

In Christ Jesus neither circumcision nor uncircumcision has any value. The only thing that counts is faith expressing itself through love (Galatians 5:6).

1. According to this verse, does circumcision or uncircumcision have any value?

2. In the same vein, do any of our religious practices have any value in light of the commands of God?

3. What is the only thing that counts in this life?

You, my brothers, were called to be free. But do not use your freedom to indulge the sinful nature; rather, serve one another in love. The entire law is summed up in a single command: "Love your neighbor as yourself" (Galatians 5:13,14).

1. What were we called to be?

2. How are we to use our freedom?

3. How does Paul sum up the entire law?

4. What then is the fundamental reason that man could not keep the law?

Let no debt remain outstanding, except the continuing debt to love one another, for he who loves his fellowman has fulfilled the law. The commandments, "Do not commit adultery," "Do not murder," "Do not steal," "Do not covet," and whatever other commandment there may be, are summed up in this one rule: "Love your neighbor as yourself." Love does no harm to its neighbor. Therefore love is the fulfillment of the law (Romans 13:8-10).

1. What is the only debt we are to have outstanding?

2. He who loves his fellowman has fulfilled what?

3. What one rule sums up all the other commandments?

4. Does love do any harm to its neighbor?

5. Therefore, what is love the fulfillment of?

We know that we have passed from death to life, because we love our brothers. Anyone who does not love remains in death (1 John 3:14).

1. How do we know that we have passed from death to life?

2. If we do not love our brother, what does this verse say that we remain in?

3. Therefore, is it possible for a lost person to love his brother as Christ loved us?

4. What then can we conclude about our love as Christians for others? Where does this love come from?

Dear friends, let us love one another, for love comes from God. Everyone who loves has been born of God and knows God. Whoever does not love does not know God, because God is love (1 John 4:7,8).

1. What does John tell us to do?

2. Where does this love for one another come from?

3. What does he conclude about those who love others?

4. What does he conclude about those who do not love?

5. How does he define love?

6. For those who are born again and love others, what are they expressing to the world around them?

> *We love because he first loved us. If anyone says, "I love God," yet hates his brother, he is a liar. For anyone who does not love his brother, whom he has seen, cannot love God, whom he has not seen. And he has given us this command: Whoever loves God must also love his brother* (1 John 4:19-21).

1. Why do we love, according to this passage?

2. If anyone says he loves God, yet hates his brother, what does John conclude about that person?

3. Is it possible for someone not to love his brother, whom he has seen, and then to love God, whom he has not seen, according to this passage?

4. What is the command that John gives us?

5. Can we love others apart from knowing and abiding in God's love for us?

When God the Holy Spirit comes to live in you it means that you now have a new mind, new desires, and a new will, "for it is God who is at work in you, both to will and to work for His good pleasure" (Philippians 2:13 NASB). God desires to express His love and forgiveness to others through you.

God's love expressed through His people crosses every boundary, hurdles every obstacle, and resolves every conflict among men. Our secret for continually giving love to others is to continually be receiving God's love for us. Only as we remain rooted and established in the depths of God's love and grace that surpasses all knowledge will we be able to pass on that love to others.

God's Command:	Love one another, even as I have loved you (with 1 Corinthians 13 love) (John 13:34,35 NASB).
God's Promise:	Being confident of this, that he who began a good work in you will carry it on to completion until the day of Christ Jesus (Philippians 1:6).
	I can do all things through Him who strengthens me (Philippians 4:13 NASB).
God's Provision:	It is God who is at work in you, both to will and to work for His good pleasure (Philippians 2:13 NASB).
God's Protection:	Never will I leave you; never will I forsake you (Hebrews 13:5).

The following is a suggested prayer:

Father, apart from You I cannot be patient, loving, or kind or free from envy and strife, but with You I can do all things. I claim by faith that because You commanded me to love, I can trust You to teach me to love with Your heart, think with Your mind, and see others through Your eyes. Help me, Father, to be filled with the knowledge of the height, depth, width, and length of Your love for me, and to allow this love to overflow into the lives of others. Amen.